Activities for 3-5 year olds

Families

Brilliant Publications Linda Mort & Janet Morris

We hope you enjoy using this book. If you would like further information on other titles published by Brilliant Publications, please write to the address given below.

Note: to avoid the clumsy 'he/she', the child is referred to throughout as 'she'.

Dedication
To Jeffrey, Leonie, Alexander, Benjamin, David, Andrew and Daniel.

Published by Brilliant Publications, The Old School Yard, Leighton Road, Northall, Dunstable, Bedfordshire LU6 2HA

Written by Linda Mort and Janet Morris
Illustrated by Virginia Gray

Printed in Malta by Interprint Limited

© Linda Mort and Janet Morris
ISBN 1 897675 37 2

The Publisher accepts no responsibility for accidents arising from the activities described in this book.

The rights of Linda Mort and Janet Morris to be identified as authors of this work has been asserted by them in accordance with the Copyright, Designs and Patents Act 1988.

First published 1998
10 9 8 7 6 5 4 3 2 1

All rights reserved. No part of this publication may be reproduced, stored in a retrieval system, or transmitted in any form or by any means, electronic, mechanical, photocopying or otherwise, without the prior consent of the copyright owner. Applications for the copyright owners' written permission to reproduce any part of this publication should be addressed to the publisher.

Contents

	page
Introduction	4

Language and literacy
Your address, please?	5
Who's who?	6
Something in this room …	7
Family library	8
What's been happening?	9
A big adventure	10
Family feelings	11

Mathematics
Tommy Thumb	12
What's your number?	13
Off to bed!	14
Who's the tallest?	15
The weekly shop	16
What's on tonight?	17
What do they need?	18

Personal and social development
I promise …	19
Best behaviour	20

Creative development
An eye for detail	21
Family fun	22
Morning sounds	23

Physical development
On the move!	24
Busy families	25

Knowledge and understanding of the world
I look like …	26
Mummy has a baby inside!	27
Off to the shops	28
'Storey' time	29
Family favourites	30
Town planning	31
Where shall we go?	32

Introduction

The family is the microcosm of a child's world. In a nurturing family environment, a child first encounters all the experiences necessary in order to develop fully. 'Families' is an ideal early years theme, guaranteeing maximum motivation, as children immediately respond to discovering that, although they have a unique place in the world, they still share much in common with others. Because of the wide diversity of family lifestyles, every effort has been made in this book to be inclusive, and to avoid stereotyping. Sensitivity to your children's circumstances will ensure that only occasional minimal adaptation of the activities will be necessary for all children to benefit to the full.

The activities are organized to work within the framework of QCA's Desirable Learning Outcomes and take into account the child's developing intellectual, social and physical skills, focusing upon ideas that will encourage the growth of a positive self-image and a positive attitude to those around her.

Try to adopt a 'play' approach as much as possible, and be flexible. Whatever the focus of any activity, the child will be learning all kinds of things from it and much will depend on your starting point. Always start from what the children already know, and their interests. You should be able to adapt all the activities in this book to work with either individual children or a small group, without too much problem.

The book uses materials which are likely to be readily available within your class or group's location, or which can be easily gathered or collected from the children's families or carers.

All of the activities are designed to give the children confidence and feelings of achievement which, in turn, will become effective tools for learning.

Your address, please?

What children should learn
Language and literacy – to learn to recite their names and addresses.

What you need
Two A4 sized pieces of card; two identical shopping catalogues; scissors; glue; items for 'catalogue office' home corner: eg small cardboard boxes, felt-tipped pens and pencils, writing pad, two telephones, an expired credit/debit card; chairs (for pretend vans).

Activity
Fold one of the A4 cards in half, widthways. Cut out six items from one of the catalogues and stick them on the card (three on either side of the fold). Number the items 1 to 6 and give each item a price (in pounds only). Cut the second piece of card into six and stick on six identical items, cut from the second catalogue (do not number them). Let the children take turns to choose an item to buy from the numbered card (the catalogue). The child telephones the catalogue office, describes the item to the telephonist and gives the number of the item. The telephonist writes down the item's number, and must ask for the caller's name and address, and write this down, using her own level of emergent writing. Other children could play being packers and the delivery drivers, delivering the items (the small cards), packed in boxes, to the children who ordered them.

Extension
Let the children send cards or short messages to their families (ask parents for a small donation towards the cost of the stamps).

Talk about
Talk about how important it is to know our names and addresses, and all the different places our names and addresses are kept, and why.

Who's who?

What children should learn

Language and literacy – to read the first names and surnames of family members.

What you need

Photocopier; sheets of A4 white paper; stapler; felt-tipped pens, wax crayons and pencils.

Activity

Send home a short letter, asking for the first names and surnames of people living in the family home. Explain that this is in order to teach the children to read the names. Make a book for each child, with one sheet of A4 paper for each member of the family. Fold the sheets 12 cm along from the left-hand side, and staple together. Cut off the remaining 6 cm, on the right-hand side of each sheet, retaining just one page at the back, which should protrude to the right (see illustration). Ask the children to draw one family member on each page, drawing only on the right-hand pages, and to write (or copy or overwrite) the first name of each person at the bottom of each page. If all the people share the same surname, this should be written on the last, protruding page. If the people have different surnames, these may be written underneath the first names on each page. On the last, protruding page, the children may write 'My family'.

Extension

Write each child's first name, middle name (if any), and surname on separate, small pieces of card. Sit the children in pairs or threes and let them 'pool' their name cards between them. Each child should find her own cards, and put them side-by-side, in order.

Talk about

Try mixing up the children's first names and surnames for fun! Talk also about 'initials', and see if the children can tell you their initials.

Something in this room ...

What children should learn
Language and literacy – to develop an awareness of initial sounds.

What you need
Shopping catalogues; scissors; sugar paper; glue; long-armed stapler.

Activity
Make a large book from the sugar paper, with one page for each room in a house (eg living room, kitchen, bathroom, two or three bedrooms). Cut the top of the book into the shape of a roof. Draw a family on the front cover, and tell the children the family's name (eg 'the Spicer family'). Say that one of the family's favourite games is 'I spy', and that this book shows all the rooms in the family's house. Cut out catalogue pictures of items belonging to the various rooms. To begin with, stick just two items on each page, and play 'I spy' with the children (focusing on initial sounds). As the children become confident with the game, add a new item to each page every few days.

Extension
Tell the children that the Spicer family go on special family outings to different places (eg to the shops, park, zoo, beach, etc). Make another book, called 'Something in this place', and stick in pictures cut from magazines, brochures, etc.

Talk about
Ask the children whether they play 'I spy' at home with their families. As you show each page in the book, ask the children whether they have similar items in their rooms at home, and whether they can think of other items beginning with the same sounds.

Family library

What children should learn

Language and literacy – to become aware of different kinds of books.

What you need

A variety of children's and adults' books, both fiction and non-fiction (eg cookery, travel, hobbies, etc); a roll of wallpaper; scissors; paints; newspaper.

Activity

Unroll the wallpaper and cut off a piece three metres in length. Roll it in the opposite direction to flatten it, and place it on the newspaper-covered floor, with a weight in each corner. Ask the children to paint pictures of a family (head and shoulders only), consisting of two grandparents, a mother, father, two teenage children (boy and girl), two five-year-old children (boy and girl) and a baby. When the faces have dried, ask the children, in turn, to place a book that they think the person would enjoy in front of each 'face'.

Extension

Repeat the activity, using magazines, video boxes or empty CD covers.

Talk about

Talk about the children's favourite books, both story books and 'finding-out' books. Ask about the different interests, hobbies and jobs of members of the children's families, and talk about how people like to read books to find out more about activities they enjoy. Encourage non-stereotypical thinking in the children when asking them to choose books for each member of the 'wallpaper family'. Tell them about people you know with unusual and interesting hobbies, eg a trainspotting grandmother.

What's been happening?

What children should learn
Language and literacy – to develop an awareness of how news and activities can be recorded in personalized booklets.

What you need
A large brightly decorated 'News Book'; paper; felt-tipped pens or crayons; stapler.

Activity
At the beginning of the week, ask parents to write in the 'News Book' about any activity the family has enjoyed over the weekend. This information can initially be followed up by the teacher using relevant stories and games. After a few weeks, use the information to make an individual news book for each child which can be used as a simple reading book. The illustrations could be done either by the teacher or the child, so long as the child is able to use the picture clues as an aid to reading. The book can then be proudly taken home to read to parents and family members.

Extension
Sometimes use the individual books in the library area for 'shared reading' and to hold up at news time, to encourage shy children to stand up in front of a group of children.

Talk about
Did the children see any of their classmates while out with their families? Could they read any names of places while they were on their outings – eg those of popular restaurants and fast-food outlets?

A big adventure

What children should learn

Language and literacy – to listen carefully and use a growing vocabulary.

What you need

No special requirements.

Activity

Ask the children to sit in a big circle on the floor. Explain how you are all going to make up a family adventure story. Start the story about an imaginary family, leaving out the end of a sentence for the first child to fill in. For example: 'Pablo lived with his mummy and baby sister in a small house on the edge of some woods. One day, he decided to … ' Bounce the story back and forth between each child and the adult, with the adult taking every other turn to keep the story moving. If a child is particularly shy, offer the opportunity of just filling in one word at the end of the sentence until her confidence gradually increases.

Extension

Turn the story into a simple illustrated book to read to other children or to use in a class assembly.

Talk about

What exciting things might happen in a family adventure? Did the children meet any monsters, dragons or wild animals? Did the car break down in the middle of nowhere?

Family feelings

What children should learn

Language and literacy – to put into words their thoughts and feelings about their families.

What you need

Five paper plates; felt-tipped pens; kitchen-roll tubes; scissors; sticky tape.

Activity

Draw faces on each plate, showing happy, sad, cross, frightened and surprised expressions. Cut the tubes into pieces, each 30 cm long. Attach each piece to a plate, with sticky tape, so that the plate may be held up like a mask. Ask the children to sit in a circle and put the plates in the middle of the circle, on the floor. Ask each child in turn to choose a plate, hold it up, and say: '_____ (name of family member) makes me feel happy (etc) when s/he _____.'

Extension

Play the same game, this time asking each child to say: '_____ (name of family member) feels happy when I _____.'

Talk about

Talk about how, in all families, people feel happy, sad, etc for many different reasons. Ask the children how they help a member of their family to feel better when they need cheering up. Ask the children whether other family members say 'sorry' to them, if necessary, and whether the children say 'sorry', too.

Tommy Thumb

What children should learn

Mathematics – to develop an awareness of conservation of number in relation to fingers.

What you need

The words of the traditional song 'Tommy Thumb' as follows:
>Tommy Thumb, Tommy Thumb,
>Where are you?
>Here I am, here I am,
>How do you do?

(repeat the verse, replacing 'Tommy Thumb' with 'Peter Pointer', 'Finger Tall', 'Ruby Ring', 'Baby Small' and 'Fingers All'); gloves and mittens.

Activity

Sing the song with the children, asking them to raise the appropriate finger on one hand for each verse. Explain that the 'finger people' are brothers and sisters in the 'finger family'. Ask the children to count how many finger people are in the 'family' using their fingers when they are both 'spread out' and also 'squashed together'.

Extension

Let each child, in turn, put a glove on one hand and spread out and squash together her fingers. Ask how many people are in the 'finger family'. Ask each child to remove the glove, and to replace it with a mitten. Ask the child to notice how only 'Tommy Thumb' is spread out on his own, while his brothers and sisters are all squashed together. Ask again how many people there are in the finger family.

Talk about

Talk about how many people there are in the children's families. Ask whether the number changes, whether the family members stand spread out or squashed together.

What's your number?

What children should learn
Mathematics – to recite, read and record telephone numbers.

What you need
Two telephones; paper; pencils; children's personal details cards (containing their telephone number).

Activity
Sit a pair of children opposite one another, with a telephone each. Say that they must telephone one another, to invite each other to play. Before each child uses the telephone, show each one their personal details card containing their telephone number. Help each child to read and/or recite their number, and to overwrite or copy it on to paper. The children should then exchange numbers, and take turns to telephone each other.

Extension
Show the children, if possible, their numbers in a telephone directory. Talk abut such numbers as '999', '100', the speaking clock, etc. Emphasize that children should make telephone calls only with their parents' knowledge.

Talk about
Ask the children who telephones them, and who they like to telephone. What do the children say if they answer the telephone? Do the children use telephone boxes? Why is it very important always to replace the receiver?

Off to bed!

What children should learn
Mathematics – to use the terms 'single', 'double', 'top', 'bottom', 'up', 'down', 'upper' and 'lower'.

What you need
Five long, thin cartons (eg for bread-sticks); glue; two kitchen-roll tubes; white paper; scissors; five small dolls; one miniature doll; fabric; a toothpaste carton; a felt-tipped pen.

Activity
Cut the white paper into rectangles to fit the long, thin cartons, and stick one rectangle on one side of each carton, to represent a sheet. Stick two cartons side-by-side, to make a double bed. Cut the tube into four pieces, each 15 cm long. Glue the tube pieces to two cartons, to make a bunk bed. Cut the toothpaste carton in half, to make a cot, sticking a small piece of card at the bottom end of the cot. Cut the fabric into five blankets (three single, one double and one tiny blanket for the cot). Let the children play 'Off to bed!', putting the dolls to bed in the cot and the single, double and bunk beds.

Extension
Let the children use cartons and circles cut from card to make a 'single-decker' and a 'double-decker' bus.

Talk about
Ask the children whether they sleep in a single, double or bunk bed. Ask if they would like to try changing the kind of bed they sleep in, and why. Ask why a baby should not sleep in the top bunk bed.

Who's the tallest?

What children should learn

Mathematics – to practise putting pictures of members of the family in order of size.

What you need

Dolls and toys; narrow rectangles of paper cut into different sizes; felt-tipped pens; photographs or pictures of families.

Activities

Ask the children to sort the dolls and toys in height order. Let the children look at your pictures of families and pick out the tallest and the shortest person. Give the children some different-sized rectangles of paper. Ask the children to pretend that each piece of paper is a member of their family. Ask each child to put their pieces of paper in size order, side-by-side. Draw a circle for the head, touching the top of the paper, and let the children draw the facial features and the rest of the body with the feet touching the bottom of the rectangle.

Can the children draw the baby of the family first (if there is one) followed by themselves, older brothers, sisters, mummy and daddy in order of height?

Extension

Ask the children to put themselves into pretend families in the classroom standing in order of height, in front of the rest of the class.

Talk about

Can the children use mathematical language to chat about their families? For example: 'I am taller than the baby but shorter than mummy.'

The weekly shop

What the children should learn

Mathematics – to appreciate how much food is bought on a family shopping trip.

What you need

A willing volunteer; a week's shopping for an average-sized family.

Activity

Ask a willing parent/teacher, from a family of four or five, to bring in his/her weekly shopping before taking it home. Have the children unpack it very carefully, and sort it into sets of similar items, eg fruit, vegetables, biscuits, cakes, etc.

Extension

Ask the children to use emergent writing and pictures from food catalogues, eg cash-and-carry magazines, to make up their own shopping lists.

Talk about

Discuss how often the children accompany parents on their weekly shopping trip. Can they remember how many loaves of bread, boxes of cereal, eggs, etc are needed? Which foods are healthy and which foods should only be eaten in small quantities?

What's on tonight?

What children should learn

Mathematics – to develop time-telling skills.

What you need

A copy of a television magazine; a large teaching clock with movable hands; a working clock with large, clear numbers and hands; a clock stamp; paper.

Activity

Send a letter home to parents asking them to look at a TV guide and to choose a favourite programme for each member of the family that begins on the hour. On receiving this information, help the children to make a mini, personalized TV guide with a clock showing the time of the programme and a picture of the family member watching television. The guide might look effective in the format of a zigzag book.

Extension

Make a pictogram to show the favourite programmes watched by mothers, fathers, siblings and the children themselves.

Talk about

What time are most children's programmes shown? Do the children watch television at the weekend? Are there some programmes all the family likes to watch? Why is it not good to watch too much television? What family activities could they be doing instead?

What do they need?

What children should learn

Mathematics – to develop an understanding of one-to-one correspondence.

What you need

Ten multi-cultural dolls; ten small teddies; ten nappies; ten bottles; ten babygros; magazine pictures of people.

Activity

Cut out pictures from magazines to represent the mummies and daddies from four families. Pretend that ten new babies have been born into these families – a single baby to one family, twins, triplets and quads to the other three families. Set out the dolls next to the pinned-up pictures of the parents in groups of one, two, three and four. Can the children sort the correct number of nappies, bottles, babygros and teddies to each family group?

Extension

Make a chart showing the number of bottles, nappies, teddies and babygros needed by each family.

Talk about

Discuss the needs of a new baby in terms of how many bottles and babygros she will require. Compare with the quantities of clothes, toys, etc needed by the children in the class.

I promise ...

What children should learn
Personal and social development – to develop an awareness of how to help at home.

What you need
Card; felt-tipped pens and crayons; magazine pictures of different rooms in the house with 'messy' items added in felt-tipped pen.

Activity
Look at the magazine pictures with the children: ask them what needs to be picked-up and tidied in each room. Can the children relate the rooms in the pictures to those in their own homes? What could they do to tidy their homes, eg pick up the towels in the bathroom and put dirty washing in the wash basket. Make a promise card for each child to take home to show her parents, eg: 'I promise to tidy my toys before I go to bed.' These can be illustrated by the children and put in envelopes addressed to the parents. The parents might send back a note the following day to say whether the promise has been carried out!

Extension
Perhaps the families make special preparations when visitors are coming to stay, eg at Christmas. Make promise cards for these occasions.

Talk about
What would happen if nobody tidied up or washed the dishes? Does each member of the family have a special job to do to help keep the house straight?

Best behaviour

What children should learn

Personal and social development – appropriate behaviour when on a family outing.

What you need

Props, eg a shopping basket, tins of food; 'litter', eg crisp/sweet packets.

Activity

Tell the children that you are going to act out some little plays about when they go out with their families. Choose a child to be the mother/father. Swap roles. The adult pretends to be the child who forgets to behave well, eg scatters the litter after a picnic, runs across the road on a shopping trip, or wanders away from mummy/daddy, makes lots of noise in the library and rustles crisp packets at the cinema/theatre. The child who is the 'parent' advises her what she should be doing.

Extension

Help pairs of children to make up little plays about the correct way to behave in these situations. Check with parents to see if the role play has had any effect on behaviour!

Talk about

Discuss what is wrong with the behaviour of the 'forgetful' child in terms of both personal safety (on the shopping trip), annoying other people (in the library/cinema/theatre) and being a danger to animals (they might choke on the picnic litter).

An eye for detail

What children should learn

Creative development – to develop their powers of observation.

What you need

Collage materials, including different-coloured wools and scraps of material; glue; felt-tipped pens; paper; paints; protective clothing.

Activity

Ask the children to bring in one photograph of themselves and one photograph of another child in their family. This could be a cousin if there are no siblings. Help the children to make collage pictures using relevant coloured eyes, hair, clothes, etc. Make the pictures look as similar as possible to the photographs in terms of appearance.

Extension

Display the collage pictures and the pairs of photographs in different parts of the room. Can the rest of the children match the pictures to the correct photographs?

Talk about

Discuss the similarities and differences between pairs of pictures. What do the children have in common? Are the smiles similar? Is the hair the same colour? Can they tell from the photographs who is older?

Family fun

What children should learn

Creative development – to use a range of collage materials and photographs to illustrate the hobby of one member of the family.

What you need

Individual photographs of faces of family members and the teacher; paper (different colours); glue; collage materials; felt-tipped pens or crayons.

Activity

Tell the children one of your hobbies, eg tennis, and discuss how you might make a special picture using a photograph of your face, white paper for your tennis clothes and string for the tennis racket. Let the children help compose this picture as a group before making a photo-picture of one member of their own family. For example, mummy might like to go bowling, big sister might go to ballet. Tell the children to stick the head near the top of the paper. Have a wide range of collage materials and coloured paper to make the clothes and any equipment. The children can draw in extra details with felt-tipped pens or crayons.

Extension

Use pictures of faces cut from magazines and collage materials to make pictures of imaginary families pursuing different activities.

Talk about

What do members of a child's family like to do after school and at the weekends? Are there any activities that everyone joins in together, eg swimming or going for a walk?

Morning sounds

What children should learn

Creative development – to create and respond to sounds heard in the home.

What you need

Alarm clock, or snatch of recorded music to represent a clock radio; small plastic washing-up bowl; plastic jug; water; cups, bowls, spoons; instruments: eg drums, wood blocks, glockenspiel or xylophone; a large floor space; chairs for half the group.

Activity

Divide the group in half. Sit one group on chairs on one side of the space. Ask the other group to sit on the floor in the remaining space. Ask the children to think of the sounds they hear at home during the course of a busy morning, perhaps on a Saturday. Ask the children for their ideas on how to recreate these sounds, using mainly their voices and percussion instruments. Ask the seated children to make the sound effects, while the rest of the children mime appropriate actions. Suggested sound effects and related actions could be:

Sound effect	Mimed actions
'snoring' by children	sleeping
alarm clock	stretching and yawning
water poured from jug into bowl	getting washed
drum beats	walking downstairs
cups, bowls and spoons being moved	preparing breakfast
humming loudly	vacuuming the carpet
'ringing' sounds	answering telephone
glockenspiel or xylophone 'doorbell'	answering door
wood blocks	closing door

Extension

Let the children make sound effects for and mime to well-known stories about families, such as *Red Riding Hood*, *The Three Billy Goats Gruff*, etc.

Talk about

Ask the children to discuss the sounds they like and dislike at home, and to say why. Which noises are quiet and which are loud?

On the move

What children should learn

Physical development – to learn to carry small items of furniture and equipment safely.

What you need

Home-corner furniture (eg small table, chairs, cot, etc); plastic cups or beakers; plastic plates; cushions; a large floor space.

Activity

Move certain items from the home-corner into one corner of a large floor space. Choose only small, light items that one or two children can carry easily and safely. Tell the children that all the items are in a big 'removal van', and that they must carry the items carefully into the 'new house' (another area of the floor space). Show the children the correct way to carry a chair, and how to co-operate in pairs in carrying a table or cot. See how many cups, beakers, plates or cushions each child can carefully carry piled in a tower (not too high).

Extension

Bring in, or show pictures of, items designed to help transport objects, eg a wheeled chair-stacker, a shopping trolley, supermarket trolley, golf bag, etc.

Talk about

Have any of the children ever moved house? What did they do to help? Have any of the children ever helped to move furniture before decorating the house? Talk about heavy and light objects and how many items need more than one person to help move them. Talk about bending at the knees to lift heavy objects.

Busy families

What children should learn
Physical development – to mime actions associated with family life.

What you need
Shopping catalogues; scissors; glue; card; a draw-string bag.

Activity
Make a card for each room in the house, sticking appropriate items on each card, eg hall (show a flight of stairs), kitchen, living room (with dining and seating areas), bathroom, bedroom. Make a card representing a garden. Put the cards in a draw-string bag. Gather the children together. Ask each child, in turn, to choose a card from the bag and to mime an action associated with that room (or garden). Before miming the action, sing the following song to the tune of 'Tommy Thumb': '_____ _____ (child's first name and surname), _____ _____ (child's first name and surname, again), Where are you?' The child should sing in reply: 'I am in the _____ (name of room). Watch what I do!'

Extension
Place up to six household objects on a tray. Ask each child in turn to choose an item mentally, and to mime using that item. The audience must guess the item, and say in which part of the house it would likely be used.

Talk about
Ask the children to think about which activities require the most and the least effort. Which activities require bending, stretching, lifting, carrying, digging, pushing or pulling? Are there any activities that are dangerous (eg climbing on furniture, etc).

I look like ...

What children should learn

Knowledge and understanding of the world – to notice similarities and differences in appearance between themselves and a parent.

What you need

Paper; pencils; crayons or felt-tipped pens; a hand-mirror; photographs of children's parents.

Activity

Note: use sensitivity if you have adopted or fostered children in your group. Ask each child to look at the photograph of one of their parents, and to look at themselves in the mirror. Discuss with each child in which ways they look the same as their parent and in which ways they look different. Each child should fold his paper in half, and draw his parent on one side, and herself on the other. Mention each feature, one by one, as the child draws, eg hair, eyes, ears, lips, hands, size, body shape, etc.

Extension

Cut out individual faces of the members of two different families, from a magazine, and see if the children can sort them into the correct families.

Talk about

Discuss the similarities and differences in hair between each child and her parent, in terms of colour, length, style (curly or straight), etc. Do they have the same colour eyes? Does the child's parent ever wear eye make-up and/or lipstick, or a nose-stud or ear-rings? Does the child's parent wear rings and/or nail varnish?

Mummy has a baby inside!

What children should learn

Knowledge and understanding of the world – to begin to appreciate how a baby grows inside a mother's body.

What you need

A pregnant mother; photographs of stages of development in the womb; photographs of new-born babies and babies of about a year old; dolls; a tape measure; sugar paper; felt-tipped pens.

Activity

Ask a pregnant mother to make regular visits to see the children, perhaps once a month from about five months of pregnancy. Let the children see how her body is growing in size as the baby grows inside. Each time she visits, show them a photograph of how the baby is developing inside the womb, and hold up a doll of about the same size. Measure the mother's waistline each time, and keep a simple record on sugar paper.

Extension

Make a doll display to show the approximate size of the baby at six months, seven months, eight months and nine months of pregnancy. Compare new-born size baby clothes with the clothes the children are wearing.

Talk about

Discuss what the baby will be able to do when it is new-born and when it is a year old. Chat about babies being able to hear songs and music while still in the womb. Sing favourite songs for her to hear (not too loudly!).

Off to the shops

What children should learn

Knowledge and understanding of the world – to use a remote-control device to make a car go forwards, backwards, left and right.

What you need

A sturdy remote-control car or roamer (decorated as a car); paper; felt-tipped pens; boxes; glue; scissors; sticky tape; play people.

Activity

Make a miniature town using boxes for shops and houses. Use a felt-tipped pen to draw roads on paper. Make sure that the roads are wide enough for the vehicle. Ask the children to plan a route from a chosen spot to the shops, verbalizing the journey, eg: 'I need to go along the main road and then turn left to get to the fruit shop.' Stick play people in the car with sticky tape, to indicate the number of people in each family. The children could write down their car number plate to be stuck, in turn, on the back of the remote vehicle.

Extension

Try using a blindfold on the child operating the vehicle, with another child giving directions. Ask the children to try to direct the driver when the family next goes to the shops.

Talk about

Which shops are most visited by the children in the class? What are the reasons? Has the shop got a big car park or a bakery with freshly baked bread and biscuits?

'Storey' time

What children should learn

Knowledge and understanding of the world – to know about different types of family homes.

What you need

Food cartons and packets; scissors; glue; felt-tipped pens; pictures of bungalows, houses (detached and semi-detached) and blocks of flats; sticky tape.

Activity

Cut open the packets etc, and flatten them. Reassemble them inside out and secure the edges with sticky tape, before the children use them. In this way they will be able to draw doors and windows, with 'families' looking through them, on a plain background. Show the children the pictures of bungalows, detached and semi-detached houses, and blocks of flats. Ask the children to select suitably-sized packets to make a 'street' of different kinds of family homes. They should estimate how many people could live in each type of home, and draw that number of people looking through the windows of their homes.

Extension

Make caravans, houseboats, tents and a palace or a castle.

Talk about

Ask the children whether they live in a one-storey or two-storey home, or a block of flats. Why do some elderly and/or disabled people like to live in bungalows or ground-floor maisonettes? Have the children heard about any family living in a palace? What do they think it would be like to live in a palace? How would it be different?

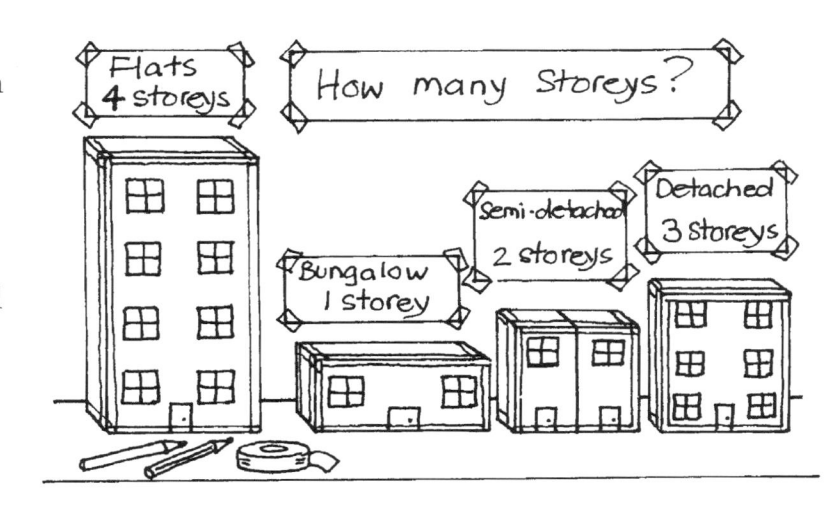

Family favourites

What children should learn

Knowledge and understanding of the world – to develop understanding that parents and grandparents were once children.

What you need

Photocopier and paper; sugar paper; felt-tipped pens; long-armed stapler.

Activity

Send home a letter, asking a parent and a grandparent to fill in a chart detailing the child's favourite books, toys and family games (eg 'I spy') and also those of the parent and grandparent at the same age. When the charts have been returned, make a class book, with a page for each child. Write down her favourite books, toys and games, and those of the parent and grandparent. Ask the child to draw one or two appropriate pictures for her page.

Extension

Bring in three teddy bears, one which looks very old, one which looks old and one new bear. Ask the children to put them in age order. Make three birthday cards, one for a 55-year old, one for a 30-year old and one for a new baby bear cub. Ask the children to match each card to its bear.

Talk about

Talk about how parents and grandparents were once children with tastes in books, toys and games which were sometimes similar to, different from or the same as those of children today. Ask the children what they think their own children might enjoy in the future.

Town planning

What children should learn

Knowledge and understanding of the world – to begin to understand some of the criteria used when choosing a home.

What you need

Small plastic/wooden houses; building bricks (to represent blocks of flats, bungalows, etc); a detailed road mat with schools, parks, libraries, etc marked on.

Activity

Ask the children to sit round the empty road mat. Discuss different types of buildings, such as hospitals, libraries, swimming pools, schools, etc. Point out the green spaces, discussing their possible uses, eg a park, a field for the farmer's cows, etc. Give each child a small house or other building and ask them, in turn, where they would like to position it. When all the buildings are on the mat, get each child to say, in turn, why she has chosen her particular spot. For example, it might be next to the swimming pool because she has just begun to have swimming lessons.

Extension

Using play people and small cars, let the children plan weekend activities (eg driving to the shops in the morning and going to the park in the afternoon). Extra buildings and areas could be added to the road mat by the teacher or children.

Talk about

Where would mummy choose to put her home – would she like it near the school or near the shops? Why might she not want it too near the airport?

Where shall we go?

What children should learn

Knowledge and understanding of the world – to understand the importance of brochures, maps, etc in planning an outing.

What you need

Leaflets and brochures about local places of interest suitable for young children; souvenirs from outings; bus/train tickets; entrance tickets; a large scrap-book; writing paper; family photos; gummed stars.

Activity

Write a letter to parents asking them to send in brochures and leaflets about popular local places of interest they have visited with their children and photographs they have taken on the outings. Let each child talk about where she would like to go, locating the destination on a map, discussing the best way to travel and how long the journey would take, etc. Make a scrap-book using all the brochures and photographs and leave it available for children and parents to browse through.

Extension

After discussion with the children, award each place stars out of five, with five stars representing a brilliant day out! Make a simple bar chart with the children, showing their favourite family outings.

Talk about

Discuss the information in the brochures. Why is it important to know opening and closing times? Why do some places close in the winter months and others stay open throughout the year?